HOT DOG! 8

ART TIME!

Scholastic Press
An imprint of Scholastic Australia Pty Limited (ABN 11 000 614 577)
PO Box 579 Gosford NSW 2250
www.scholastic.com.au

Part of the Scholastic Group
Sydney • Auckland • New York • Toronto • London • Mexico City
• New Delhi • Hong Kong • Buenos Aires • Puerto Rico

First published by Scholastic Australia in 2020.

Cover and internal design by Nicole Stofberg and Nicolette Treanor.

A catalogue record for this book is available from the National Library of Australia

ISBN: 978-1-74383-652-1

Typeset in YWFT Mullino.

Printed in China by Dream Colour.
Scholastic Australia's policy, in association with Dream Colour, is to use papers that are renewable and made efficiently from wood grown in responsibly managed sources, so as to minimise its environmental footprint.

10 9 8 7 6 5 4 3 2 1 26 27 28 29 30 / 2

ANH DO

ILLUSTRATED BY
DAN McGUINESS

HOT DOG! 8

ART TIME!

A Scholastic Press book
from Scholastic Australia

ONE

Hi, I'm **Hotdog**.

Right now, I'm painting my **friends** . . .

That's not what I mean!

I'm painting **pictures** of my friends.

Kev . . .

and **Lizzie**.

We all **love** painting!

I love painting friends, but Kev likes to paint pictures of . . .

FOOD!

Kev likes painting breakfast at **breakfast** . . .

lunch at **lunch** . . .

and dinner at **DINNER!**

And sometimes, he paints **all three at once!**

We wish Lizzie liked painting pictures of things like **rainbows or puppies or flowers** . . .

But Lizzie isn't into any of that **cute** stuff.

Lizzie prefers painting pictures of . . .

MONSTERS!

EEEEEEK!

Lizzie's monsters are **SO SCARY!** They look so real! And, even worse, they're **everywhere!**

It's so scary that Kev has to **shut his eyes** on the way to the bathroom.

He even closes his eyes when he's having a **midnight snack!**

It **scares** me too . . . The other night I thought I was having **a nightmare!**

But it was just a new painting that Lizzie had done of a **VAMPIRE DINOSAUR!**

Kev and I are trying to be **brave**, like Lizzie, but it **isn't** easy!

Lately we've been jumping in fright even when the **doorbell rings!**

The three of us have been working **hard** on our paintings because the local art museum is having a **contest**.

The **winner's** work will stay in the museum for all to see! How **cool** is that?!

Now we have to pick our **favourite** paintings to enter!

Kev chose his favourite burger painting, I chose a group portrait I'd done of all of us, and Lizzie chose her **SCARIEST** monster painting.

TWO

Everyone gathered in the museum, waiting for the **winner** to be announced. We were up against some **amazing** artists.

Pablo Pigasso ...

Andy Warthog . . .

. . . and **Leonardo Da Pinchy.**

Everyone seemed to like our stuff, too.

Well, not **quite** everyone . . .

But, in the end, it was **Vincent Van Crow** who took out the **big prize!**

THAT PAINTING AND THIS MOOO-SEUM ARE UDDER-LY FABULOUS.
I TOAD-ALLY AGREE.

'That's an awesome **bird** painting,' I said as we stared up at Vincent Van Crow's artwork.

'It's im-PECK-able,' said Lizzie.

'I'm hungry,' said Kev. 'Can we find something to eat?'

'How about we check out the museum first?' I said.

I **really** wanted to take a look around.

'Plus, we **HAVE** to see the Llama Lisa,' I added.

The Llama Lisa was the most famous painting **IN THE ENTIRE UNIVERSE!**

We packed our paintings onto our wagon and went for a stroll. The museum was **heaps** of fun. First, we checked out a room full of **cool** sculptures . . .

Then some **paintings** . . .

ME SO HUNGRY!

THAT GUY LOOKS LIKE HE JUST SAW MY VAMPIRE DINOSAUR PAINTING!

Next, we looked at some ancient art.
Stuff that was **REALLY** old!

YOU THINK I'M OLD? YOU SHOULD SEE MY MUMMY!

I skidded to a stop when I thought I saw a couple of **familiar** faces wandering around . . .

. . . but they just turned out to be cleaners.

Then we found an old Egyptian ruler that looked **JUST LIKE LIZZIE!**

It was so funny, we had to take a pic!

SELFIE TIME!

Lastly, we headed to the hall to see the most famous painting of all. The **Llama Lisa!**

But when we reached the hall, we found **POLICE** everywhere!

The Llama Lisa was **gone!**

SOMEONE HAD STOLEN IT!

THREE

Everyone was in a panic! How could someone have snuck in and stolen such a **famous painting?**

No-one seemed to know what to do!

'Did anyone see anything?' asked one of the police officers. 'Was anyone acting **strangely?'**

But everyone just **shrugged**. It was a mystery!

Again, everyone shrugged.

Then, suddenly, I remembered the cleaners I'd seen earlier. I was **pretty sure** they were **carrying** something out . . .

What if they weren't cleaners **at all?**

What if they were—

Rooster and Donkey!

Rooster and Donkey were a couple of bad guys who were always causing **trouble**. They stole a little girl's bike once . . . Could it have been **them** that stole the Llama Lisa?

'Quick, the camera!' I said.

'I know,' I said. 'But I need to see the photo we took earlier.'

Lizzie handed me the camera and I found the photo of us.

‘What is it?’ Lizzie asked.

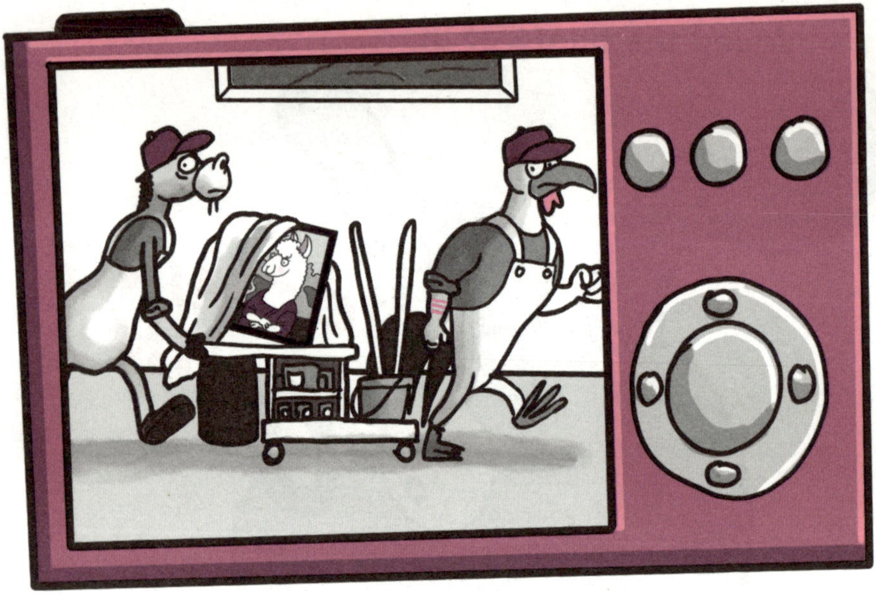

It **was** them! Posing as cleaners so they could steal the **Llama Lisa!**

'Rooster and Donkey stole the Llama Lisa!' I said.

Lizzie and Kev **raced** outside with me as we searched for any sign of the art burglars!

'Look!' I said. **'Over there!'**

Across the road, Donkey and Rooster were taking off in a van.

'They're getting **away!'** shouted Lizzie.

'Come on,' I said, jumping on the dino bike. 'Let's **chase** them!'

THAT VAN!'

As soon as Donkey and Rooster realised we were hot on their heels, they **sped right up.**

'You **can do it**, Hotdog!' yelled Kev. 'Don't let them get away!'

I pedalled as **fast** as my little legs could handle. But just as we were in with a chance of catching them . . . the van **flew** around a corner . . .

. . . and out of sight.

'Hang on, did you **see** that?' I asked.

'The bad guys getting away?' said Lizzie. 'Yes, we **all saw it.'**

'No, something fell out of the van,' I said.

Maybe it was a **clue!**

I ran over to check it out . . . but it was just a scrunched up **napkin**.

Or was it? I decided I'd better take a closer look.

Yes! It **was** a clue!

'Castle Creepy?!' said Lizzie with a squeal. 'The spookiest place on earth?! With the Rattling Bones **Ghost Train?** And the **Monster Moat?**'

'But that place shut down **ages** ago, didn't it?' I said.

'Sure did,' said Kev. 'It was such a **shame** . . .'

Lizzie and I both looked at Kev.

'But you **HATE** scary stuff,' I said. 'Just like me!'

'Oh, I never went anywhere near the **spooky** rides!' he said. 'I only ever ran in and out for the **Chocolate Spiders** and the **Eye-ball Cake Pops.**'

What would Rooster and Donkey want with a shut-down fun park? A **big, empty** space, with no-one around . . .

'That's it!' I cried. 'They must be **hiding** there! We have to go there **right now!'**

'We have to go there?' said Kev, his lip trembling.

It was true, we didn't like **scary stuff!**

'But we **also** don't like giving up,' I said. 'And there's a **famous painting** that

NEEDS RESCUING!'

FOUR

Castle Creepy was just like I remembered it. **CREEPY!**

Sure enough, we found Rooster and Donkey's van parked nearby, **hidden** amongst some trees.

We stared up at the castle . . .

'There!' I said to my friends, pointing to a window in one of the highest towers. 'There's a **light** on.'

'You're right!' said Lizzie. 'Look! I think I can see Rooster's shadow!'

'There aren't enough **Chocolate Spiders** in the world to make me go in there,' said Kev.

I was really scared, too. I'd only ever been inside the Castle Creepy gates once when I was a **puppy** . . .

Mum had just bought me an 'I-scream'. I was walking through the garden . . . when **one of the plants moved!**

I sat outside the gates while everyone else had fun. I was **way too scared** to go back in!

But I wasn't going to wait outside for **THIS** mission!

'You can wait out here if you really want,' I said to Kev. 'But, remember, we can do **anything** when we're together.'

'Yeah,' said Lizzie, 'with the three of us, we have **TRIPLE** the bravery!'

At that moment, a huge bird flew by and squawked loudly.

Kev **leapt** into my arms.

'You're not going **anywhere** without me!' he cried.

We opened the gate and it made a super-creepy **CREEEEEEEEEEEEEAKING** sound!

'Just needs a bit of oil,' said Lizzie. 'Come on, you two. You can do it. Remember, **triple the bravery!**'

Kev grabbed his wagon, with our paintings sitting inside.

'We can't leave **these** behind when there are art burglars on the loose!' he said.

Lizzie led the way up the hill, past the overgrown gardens.

Come on, Hotdog, I told myself. *You must be brave. Like Lizzie. There's a painting that needs rescuing.*

I took a **deep breath** and **puffed** my chest.

This wasn't **so bad**. It was just an old rundown fun park. In the **middle of the day.**

There was **nothing to fear.**

But then **I saw it** . . .

Instantly, brave Lizzie **dashed across** in front of me . . .

. . . and kicked the head **right off the monster!**

'Not on **my** watch, buddy!' said Lizzie.

The garden monster was nothing but a robot! **A BUSTED robot!**

The yard was **nowhere** near as scary now that I knew the plants were all **just machines!**

'Let's keep moving,' said Lizzie.

When we got to the castle moat, it was filled with **robot crocodiles**.

Next to me, Kev was muttering, 'They're **just robots**, they're **just robots**.'

Lizzie pulled on the drawbridge lever . . . but nothing happened. She tried again. Nothing! It was **stuck!**

We had **no way** of getting across! What were we going to do?

I glanced over at Kev again. He seemed to be **thinking hard**. He was watching the crocodiles closely.

'I can get across,' he said, finally. 'I've worked out the **pattern**. All I have to do is **leap** over the crocodiles as they shut their mouths. Then I can get the drawbridge down.'

I was **impressed!** That was very brave of Kev! But one false move and he'd be a **robot crocodile's dinner!**

'Yep, that's what I'll do,' he said, preparing to leap.

'You can do it!' said Lizzie.

BETTER MAKE IT SNAPPY!

With that, Kev took a **flying leap** over to the first crocodile.

RL!
JUMP!
?
?

It was amazing! He was **hopping** and **bopping** to the crocodile rock! Kev leapt like a ballerina and was over the monster moat **in no time!**

He pulled on the jammed drawbridge and freed it, easily. It came down with a **THUMP!**

Lizzie and I **ran** across to our friend.

Kev looked **really** proud of himself. He was much braver than he **realised!**

And then a tiny mouse scuttled past . . .

FIVE

Inside, the castle was big and dark and dusty. There were huge paintings everywhere, with eyes that seemed to stare at us . . .

The Rattling Bones Ghost Train was on our left, covered in **cobwebs**.

The Haunted Library was on our right. Out of nowhere, a couple of books flew off the shelves and **crashed** to the floor.

Ahead, was the entrance to the **Crazy Ballroom**.

'We have to go **through** there to get to the stairs,' said Lizzie, pointing ahead.

I tried the handle, but the doors were locked. They **wouldn't budge!** Even when all three of us gave them a big strong **shove!**

How could we get in?

'Kev, Lizzie,' I said, coming up with an idea. 'If you can give me a **boost**, I'm pretty sure I can reach up and **squeeze** through that window up there.'

And with that, Lizzie helped me onto Kev's shoulders. I **reached** up and was just long enough to grab onto the window. I used **all my strength** to pull myself up and through!

Sometimes being **long** and **thin** comes in handy!

I unlocked the door and let the others into the **Crazy Ballroom**. The whole room was a **giant mirror maze!**

Some of the mirrors made us look so **funny!** And some of them made us look really, **REALLY SCARY!**

In one room it looked like there were **hundreds** of us!

Everywhere we went, **spooky** stuff kept **flying** down at us. At first we were scared . . .

But then Lizzie worked out that we could just **whack** them away!

Finally, we made it to the stairs.

'Kev, we're going to have to leave the wagon behind,' I said. 'We **can't** take it up the stairs.'

‘Okay,’ said Kev. ‘I’ll just **quickly** hide our paintings.’

We were **huffing** and **puffing**, almost at the top of the stairs, when we heard a funny sound.

'HEE-HAW!'

Hee-haw?

It was DONKEY! He'd spotted us!

'You'll **never** catch us!' he said. Then Rooster appeared and **pulled** a lever at the top of the stairs.

Suddenly, the stairs turned into a **slide!** The three of us whooshed back down, **slipping** and sliding . . .

. . . all the way to the bottom!

As hard as we tried, we just couldn't get back up the slide! It was **impossible!**

What could we do?

I remembered that the rollercoaster **looped** all the way up to the top of the castle! If we rode it, we could **jump** out at the top and **catch** Rooster and Donkey!

'Great idea!' said Kev.

For once, Lizzie looked uneasy. **Scared**, even.

'Lizzie?' I asked. 'You okay?'

'You know how I'm scared of heights?' she said. 'Well, I've **never** been on that rollercoaster. It goes too **high**.'

Lizzie was **so brave**. It was hard to imagine her being scared of anything.

All day, she had shown us how to be brave, now it was **our turn**.

'Lizzie, we can do anything together, right?' said Kev. 'Even ride the Rattling Bones Ghost Train at **Castle Creepy!**'

'Triple the bravery, remember?' I added.

We all **hopped** into the rollercoaster carts and pulled down the safety bars. As soon as we were all in, I reached over and **pulled** the lever to make it go.

It **clicked** a few times, and then . . .

THE RATTLING BONES GHOST TRAIN WAS WILD!

We flew up, down, around, forwards, backwards . . .

AAAARRGGGGGGGGGGGRRRRRRRRRRRRRRRRRRGGGGHHHHHHHHHHHHHHHHHHHHH!!!!!!!!

. . . until, **finally**, we reached the castle tower!

'This is our stop!' I called out. **'Jump!'**

We **burst** through the window, surprising Rooster and Donkey!

And there was the **Llama Lisa!**

'Give up!' said Lizzie. 'We've got you now!'

Rooster and Donkey just looked at each other and grinned.

'You've got us, **do you?'** said Rooster, **grabbing** the painting.

Then Rooster reached out and pulled another lever, and the floor beneath them **collapsed**.

A trapdoor!

'We have to **follow** them!' I said. 'Come on!'

The three of us held hands and **jumped** into the chute.

The chute was like a curling **slippery dip** that wound . . .

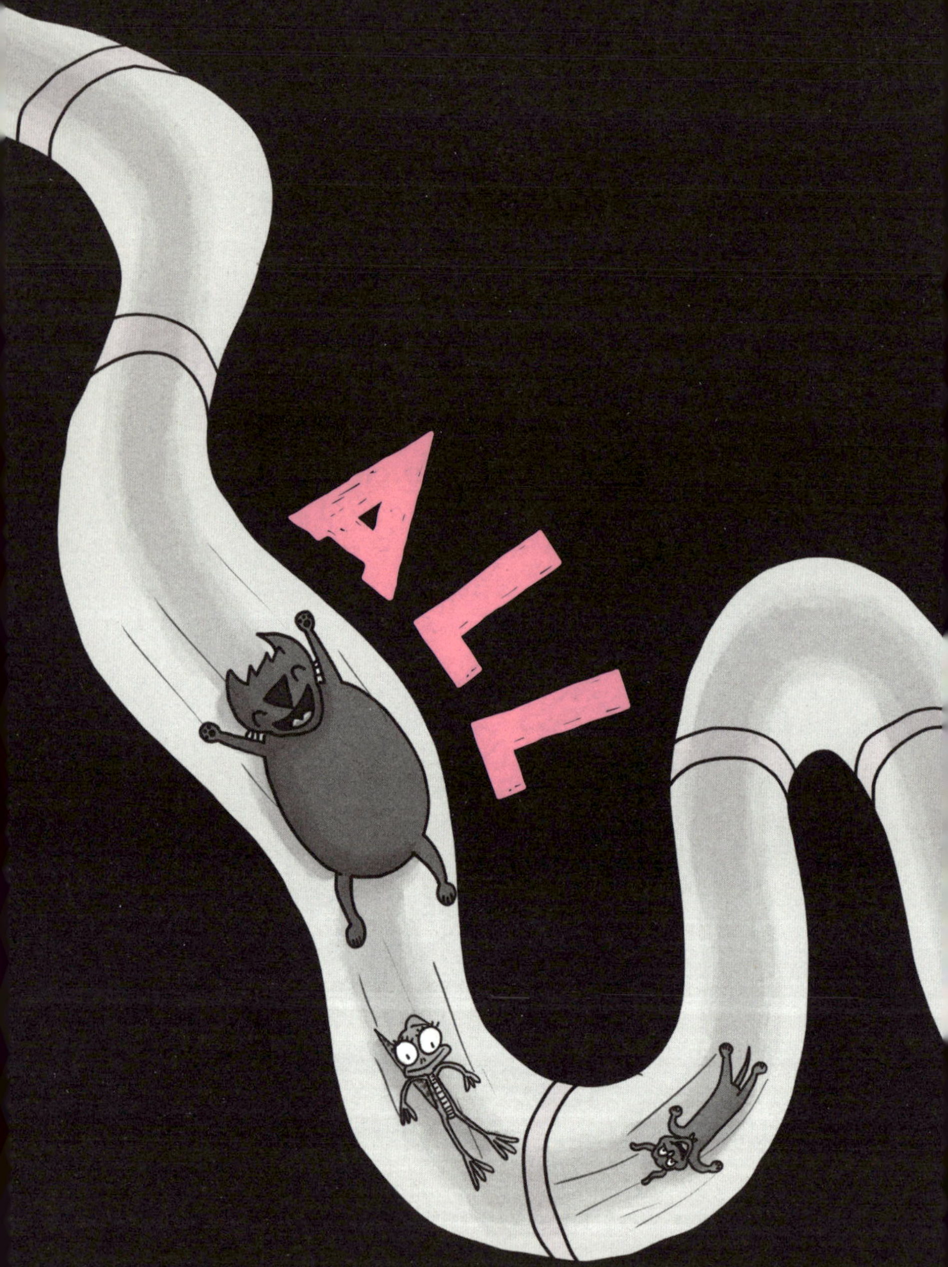
ALL

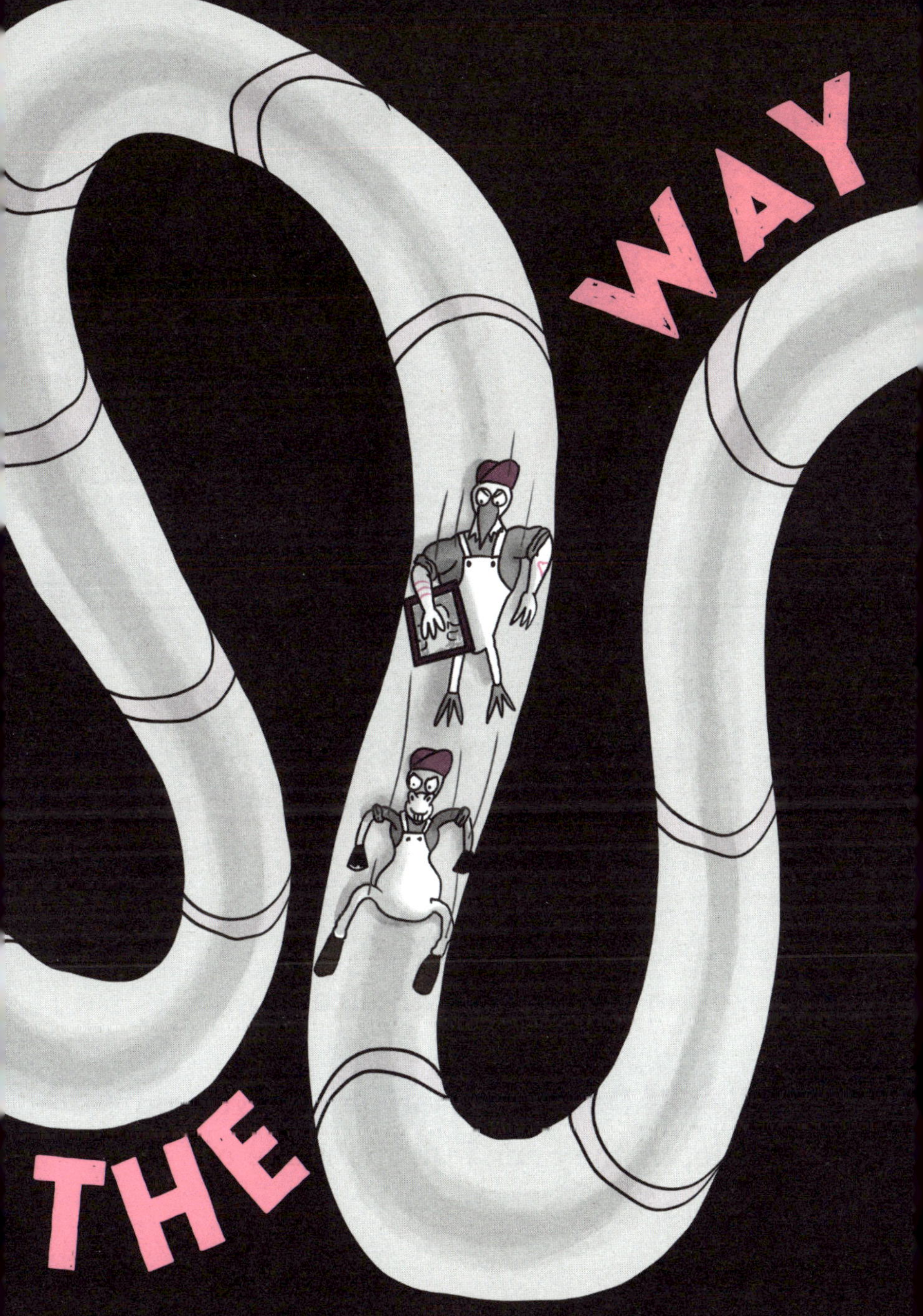
THE
WAY

. . . down to the Crazy Ballroom.

'**Quick!** Don't let them get away!' said Lizzie, as they ran into the maze of mirrors.

We chased them as fast as we could, but they were getting away from us. Had we **failed** in our rescue mission?

Then, suddenly, we heard some **terrified shrieks!**

'ARRRRRGH! HELP ME! MONSTERS! REAL MONSTERS!'

Donkey and Rooster were in the room of mirrors . . . where Lizzie's monster painting was reflected a **hundred** times!

If Kev and I weren't so used to seeing Lizzie's monster paintings, we'd have been **terrified** too!

Donkey and Rooster were **screaming** in terror! As they both tried to get away from Lizzie's monsters, they ran right **into each other!**

I **swooped** down and grabbed the Llama Lisa.

'Let's get **out** of here!' I shouted to my friends.

The three of us ran to the exit **as fast as we could.**

'Get them!' I heard Rooster shout.

Just as we **BURST** out of the ballroom doors, Rooster came flying through the air with a **HUGE, TERRIFYING** kick!

He was headed **straight for us!**

The **PAINTING** of us!

He'd been fooled and now he was **stuck!**

Next thing I knew, Donkey was coming straight for me . . . the **REAL** me!

Kev slapped his painting down over Donkey, stopping him **just in time!**

'In a bit of a **pickle?'** said Kev with a laugh, as police sirens began to wail in the distance.

I hugged my friends. **We'd done it!** We'd caught the bad guys and rescued the Llama Lisa!

SIX

So we **didn't** win the art museum contest with our paintings, but we were **REALLY BRAVE** and worked together to capture two art thieves!

Plus we **rescued** the most famous painting in the world!

Pretty cool, huh?

I love my friends!